Looking at

Animals on
PLAINS
and
PRAIRIES

Published by Raintree Steck-Vaughn Publishers,
an imprint of Steck-Vaughn Company

Series Editor Honor Head
Series Designer Hayley Cove
Picture Researcher Juliet Duff
Map Artwork Robin Carter / Wildlife Art Agency
Animal Symbols Arlene Adams

Raintree Steck-Vaughn Publishers Staff
Project Manager: Joyce Spicer
Editor: Pam Wells
Cover Design: Gino Coverty

Library of Congress Cataloging-in-Publication Data
Butterfield, Moira, 1961–
Animals on plains and prairies / Moira Butterfield.
p.   cm. — (Looking at)
Includes index.
Summary: Introduces animals that live on plains and prairies, including lions, gazelles, vultures, termites, lizards, and prairie dogs.
ISBN 0-7398-0109-0 (hardcover)
1. Grassland animals — Juvenile literature.   [1. Grassland animals.]
I. Title.   II. Series: Butterfield, Moira. 1961–   Looking at —
QL115.B88   1999
591.74 — dc21   99-17901
CIP

Printed in China
1 2 3 4 5 6 7 8 9 0 LB 02 01 00 99

Photographic credits
Frank Lane Picture Agency: 9, 12, 18, 25, 26 David Hosking, 10 E&D Hosking.
NHPA: 11 Christophe Ratier, 19 Daryl Balfour, 20 John Shaw,
22 Anthony Bannister. Oxford Scientific Films: 6 Frank Schneidermeyer,
8 Daniel J Cox, 13 Stan Osolinsk, 21 Michael Fogden, 23 Patti Murray,
27 Jen & Des Bartlett, 29 Wendy Shattil and Bob Rozinski. Planet Earth Pictures:
7 Roger de la Harpe, 14 K&K Ammann, 15 Frank Krahmer, 17 Steve Bloom,
24 William S Paton, 28 Adam Jones. Tony Stone Images: 16 Art Wolfe.
Cover credit Prairie dog: Planet Earth Pictures/Adam Jones

Looking at

Animals on
PLAINS
and
PRAIRIES

Moira Butterfield

RSVP
RAINTREE
STECK-VAUGHN
P U B L I S H E R S
A Steck-Vaughn Company

Austin, Texas

www.steck-vaughn.com

Introduction

Plains and prairies are large open spaces where there is plenty of grass but not many trees. Most plains and prairies are hot places, but a few are cold.

Animals that eat only plants live here because there is plenty of food for them to munch. They are called herbivores.

Hunting animals live here because there is lots of food for them to catch and kill. Animals that eat meat are called carnivores.

Contents

Lion

African lions sleep a lot during the day when it is hot. They are predators. Lions prowl at night when it is cool, looking for animals to chase and kill.

A family of lions is called a pride, and baby lions are called cubs. A male lion has long hair called a mane.

Zebra

Zebras live in big groups called herds. They move around the plains of southern Africa looking for grass to eat and water to drink. They all have striped coats. But each animal has its own special pattern of stripes that is different from all the other zebras.

Gazelle

Gazelles live in herds on the African plains. Lots of hunting animals like to eat them. While they move around eating grass, gazelles listen for enemies.

If they hear a noise, they sniff the air to find out if their enemies are nearby. If they need to, gazelles can run fast to escape.

Vulture

Vultures are scavengers. This means they do not hunt animals. Instead they find dead ones to eat. They can see a long way, and they can smell well, too. They spread their big wings and glide high in the sky, looking down below for food to eat.

Elephant

The African elephant is the largest animal living on land. It needs a lot of food, and it spends all day looking for grass and leaves to eat.

Baby elephants live with their mother and their aunts. If a lion comes too close, the bigger elephants chase it away.

Cheetah

The cheetah is a big cat that lives on the flat plains of Africa. It is a fierce hunter, with sharp claws and teeth. Cheetahs catch and eat other animals. They are the fastest animals in the world. A cheetah can run much faster than a person. It is as fast as a speeding car.

Giraffe

Giraffes are good at reaching up to pull leaves off the tallest trees. Drinking is more difficult because they have to reach a long way down to the water.

While a giraffe is busy drinking, it is in great danger because a crocodile could swim up and grab it.

Termite

Termites are tiny plant-eating insects that live in big groups called colonies. Each colony works together to build a mud nest that looks like a giant tower. Inside there are many, very small tunnels. This is where the termites can hide away from the hot sun.

Aardvark

The aardvark loves to eat termites. It has strong claws for ripping holes in termite nests and an extra-long tongue for licking out the insects.

The aardvark digs a burrow to hide in during the heat of the day. It closes its nostrils while it is digging to keep out dust.

Agama Lizard

Little agama lizards live in groups on the African plains. They spend their days hunting for insects or resting in the sun. When an agama lizard is scared or angry, its skin color changes. It will turn from brown to bright blue or orange.

Ostrich

The ostrich is the largest bird in the world. It lives on the African plains where there are lots of plants and insects for it to eat. It cannot fly, but it can run very fast.

It has strong legs and kicks hard if it is attacked. Ostrich eggs are big, almost round, and about the size of a football.

Prairie Dog

Prairie dogs are not real dogs. They live in big underground burrows with many tunnels. A burrow has special places for storing food and looking after babies. It also has escape tunnels. This is in case the prairie dogs are attacked by enemies or the burrow is flooded by rain.

Where They Live

This map of the world shows you where the animals live.

- lion
- zebra
- gazelle
- vulture
- elephant
- cheetah
- giraffe
- termite
- aardvark

 agama lizard

 ostrich

 prairie dog

NORTH AMERICA

SOUTH AMERICA

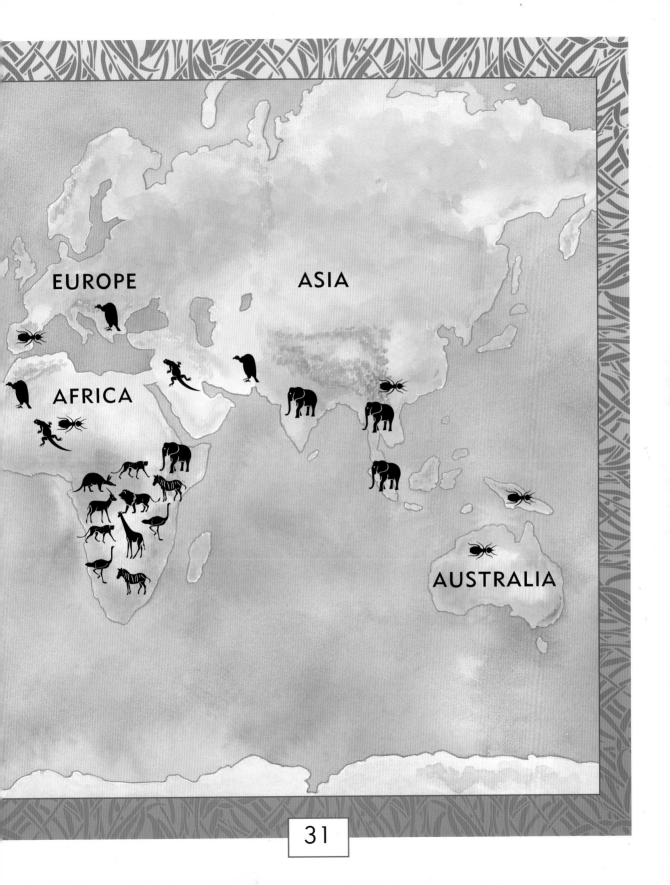

EUROPE

ASIA

AFRICA

AUSTRALIA

Index of Words to Learn